Caution!
Old Age
Ahead

*Preparing Adequately for Your Golden Years
While Still Young*

BEATRICE IJIWOLA

Summit House
Publishers

Chicago, IL

Caution! Old Age Ahead

Paperback ISBN 978-1-7356699-0-8

Published by:
Summit House Publishers
824E 43rd St Chicago IL 60653, USA

Except otherwise stated, scripture quotation is taken from the New King James Version Copyright © 1982 by Thomas Nelson, Inc. Used by permission. All rights reserved.

Printed in the USA

Dedication

To the two groups of people that will find this book helpful:

My fellow seniors (the elderly), many of whom are still hoping for a better life. Don't give up. As long as there is life, there is still hope.

And also, the younger generation: Old age is coming at you faster than you think. This book is to help you prepare adequately for it.

Acknowledgment

My deep appreciation goes to my Creator who has accompanied me through thick and thin in this journey of life. You are indeed a faithful God.

I thank all my children for their tireless contributions in making the dream of this book a living reality and for all the support they continually offer me - financially and in every other way. You all continue to make my older years joyful, blessed and fulfilling.

Special thanks to Doyin Ijiwola for his untiring efforts and encouragement over this book since I shared its vision with him in

2016. Even when I wanted to give up on the vision, he kept on pushing me towards the goal.

To those that will meet me through this book, I celebrate you ahead and charge you not to give up on whatever dream God has given you. Always remember: Winners don't quit and quitters don't win.

Contents

Foreword

The law of time perspective espoused by Dr. Edward Banfield says that the most successful people in any society are those who take the longest time period into consideration when making their day-to-day decisions. Maybe, if most people had considered the long-term effects of the actions and decisions they made in the early stages of their lives, things would have turned out much better for them today.

Changes come with time, but many of us seem unaware of the changes that are happening to us and around us. We only focus on now and live today as if tomorrow won't come. We think less of tomorrow because we've been taught tomorrow will take care of itself. We are so much engrossed with the fleeting enjoyment of the moment that we assume every day will always be the same. Nothing is the same as it used to be. Times are changing; things are getting more uncertain and difficult. Many grow into the older age regretting what they should have done but never did. It is somehow more worrisome that a lot of young people who are meant to leverage, explore and maximize the opportunities of the information age are victims of wrong choices; they are making the same mistakes as the older generation before them.

> IF MOST PEOPLE HAD CONSIDERED THE LONG-TERM EFFECTS OF THE ACTIONS AND DECISIONS THEY MADE IN THE EARLY STAGES OF THEIR LIVES, THINGS WOULD HAVE TURNED OUT MUCH BETTER FOR THEM

God has your future in mind and already made beautiful plans for you. Jeremiah 29:11 (NLT) says, *For I know the plans I have for you, says the LORD. They are plans for good and not for disaster, to give you a future and a hope.* It is, however, your responsibility to discover this plan and to seek how this spiritual reality can be translated into physical manifestation. Proverb 6:6-8 NLT gives us some insight; *Take a lesson from the ants, you lazybones. Learn from their ways and be wise. Even though they have no prince, governor, or ruler to make them work, they labor hard all summer, gathering food for the winter.*

CAUTION! OLD AGE AHEAD is a timely and resourceful guide that provides answers for all age groups and specifically for individuals who willfully desire to live happy and fulfilled golden years. This book will help reshape your perspective and challenge you to wake up to reality and act wisely with the future in mind. I have known the author, Mrs. Beatrice Ijiwola, for many years. She is enjoying her golden years and passionately desires to share insights from her experiences and those of those others. This book will surely bless you. Read, Reflect, and Take Action!

Dr. Sam Adeyemi,
Atlanta, August 2020.

Introduction

This book is an attempt to right a wrong - one that has become the mindset of many, and is being passed on from adults to children, and they to their own children when they start their own families. This wrong is a set of subtle assumptions about old age fueled by ignorance and other factors that make people live in denial and neglect while still in their prime.

People become so locked in into this wrong belief that they do not question it when things don't go their way in their latter days. Sometimes, they also don't find the need to adjust -- if it was still possible at all at that age -- or to admit their errors and point their children to the right paths, so they don't end up the same way.

I started asking such questions as I was advancing in age towards my seventies, and those questions have led to the writing of this book. I was somehow dissatisfied with the returns I have had in life regarding finances, comfort and some of my dreams in my younger years.

Why was I dissatisfied? As I looked back through the past decades of my life, I fully appreciated God for all the innumerable blessings I have enjoyed in life, but another part of me reflected on so many things that I had attempted that had produced either no result or less result than I had expected.

I recalled certain financial investments that either fizzled away and brought no returns or were taken from me. For instance, I once bought a piece of land that was confiscated from me without the money I paid being returned to me. Another property I was building up at a time was dismantled. Some other investment endeavors ended up being fruitless as well. Though I am blessed and comfortable enough in life and have enjoyed God's blessings. I couldn't help but feel that I should have greater means and possessions than I currently have now as a senior. I felt that even some of my contemporaries who didn't work as much as I have, have more assets than I do now.

I started pondering. Why did things turn out the way they did? Was it a generational curse? Was it a lack of planning? What should I have done that I did not do? My not-too-pleasant experiences prompted these questions and begged for answers.

> I FULLY APPRECIATED GOD FOR ALL THE INNUMERABLE BLESSINGS I HAVE ENJOYED IN LIFE, BUT ANOTHER PART OF ME REFLECTED ON SO MANY THINGS THAT I HAD ATTEMPTED THAT HAD PRODUCED EITHER NO RESULT OR LESS RESULT THAN I HAD EXPECTED.

Apart from my own questions, I also began to observe other older citizens from my vantage point as a senior, widow, grandmother, and a caregiver for people who are far more advanced in age than I am. I have carefully observed that many people in my age bracket are in far worse situations than I am. Many are still struggling to eke out a living when they are supposed to be eating the fruits of their hard labor of past decades. Some people in their 70s are still doing 7 to 8 hours of work every day, literally toiling to their grave. Why should this be? What went wrong during their prime years? What didn't they do right? I pondered still.

Since that time, through prayers, study, observations and reflections, augmented by my experiences and conversations in recent years as a care-giver in Chicago for aged people, I found some answers. My reason for writing this book is to share what I have learned with the hope that perhaps it might help the younger generation and others my age who are asking the same questions I had.

With the benefit of hindsight, the wrong I hope can be righted is the lack of adequate planning for the future and old age by many while they are still young. Many people of my own generation did not sow adequate seeds for their future when they were younger. They were carried away with needs and fads of the then present that they didn't take time to plan for the future that is now. As this book will show, the wrong many committed is not doing enough to invest in their future. Lack of planning and proper investment for old age is the "curse" many seniors have to battle with now at a time they ought to be enjoying the blessings that should have accrued to them by their years of labor and investments.

The argument may be that back then 30 to 40 years ago, especially in the developing world, there was little information on investments compared to now. Some that had the information then would rather have hoarded it than share it, unlike today when investment information is abundant. There are numerous seminars, presentations and contents on the internet today that can give information on

> THE WRONG I HOPE CAN BE RIGHTED IS THE LACK OF ADEQUATE PLANNING FOR THE FUTURE AND OLD AGE BY MANY WHILE THEY ARE STILL YOUNG.

investment and its opportunities. In the local church I belong to, several speakers have come to share on how to become an investor but back then, the churches we attended only allowed "spiritual things" in church. We were told no "business of the world" can be brought into the house of God. Our Christianity then taught us a lot about heaven but did not do much about how to live well on earth. We were told to prepare our souls for eternity (which is important) but we were not taught how to prepare our affairs for the sun-setting days of our lives. In hindsight, this didn't help my own generation.

However, the reality – and another reason why I wrote this book – is that despite the loads of information available to today's younger ones, many are still not taking investing in their future seriously as they should and to the level of information at their disposal. Many people in their 30s and 40s are making just the same mistakes their parents made, which will make life really tough and difficult for many of them in their older age.

My pondering therefore encompass what people of my age bracket did wrong and what our children and their own mates need to do right at this time so they will avoid the mistakes we made. How can today's young ones - professionals, business owners, and even students and the unemployed - plan for life after retirement and for old age? That is the essence of this book.

Caution! Old Age Ahead captures the need to live well while young while strategically preparing for a happy and comfortable old age. I have written this book to help you pursue this ideal and realize its essence.

CHAPTER 1

The God-Factor

Remember now your Creator in the days of your youth, Before the difficult days come, And the years draw near when you say, "I have no pleasure in them"

- The Preacher

I have lived in both the developed and developing worlds. In the United States where I live now, we have a strong credit system which allows people to engage in lifestyles that are often beyond their means. The use of debts such as credit card loans, car loans and mortgages is very prevalent. By getting by with debt, many feel they are achieving what is often referred to as the American Dream.

When you can buy a huge house with a 30-year mortgage, furnish the house on credit, get a car loan to buy a couple of cars to go with the garage, and even go shopping for clothing and accessories for yourself with a credit card to reflect your status, you may feel on top of the world – at least for the moment. You feel self-sufficient until the dream becomes a nightmare.

It is a different story in Africa where I grew up. The financial system is still developing, so there are no credit cards to live on. Many people do not have any aid to meet basic needs other than what their incomes can afford. With such levels of lack and need, people usually seek interventions from more empowered sources such as the government, non-governmental organizations and foundations that could come to their aid. They also seek intervention from God.

Africans have generally been accused by the Western world of doing too much of praying and seeking God over their problems and predicaments. We are accused of an over-emphasis on spirituality and seeking supernatural and other worldly solutions to our issues. Identifying with my African roots, I concede that we are guilty of this. But could this be because we have nowhere to turn to apart from God?

However, though I strongly recommend making God the center of your life and your source for all your supplies, I am not in support of being lazy or neglecting to do your own part in meeting your needs in the name of seeking and serving God. I am sure God Himself is not in support of this.

Is it wrong to seek divine intervention? Not at all, because God is always there to come to the aid of those that genuinely seek Him. In life, there is actually a God-factor that can be engaged to ensure that things turn out right for you. In the context of this book, the God-factor can indeed help you to live well now while also preparing you for your latter years. I can relate with this because my experience reflects it.

Remember Your Creator While Young

When I was in my twenties and thirties, although I went to church, I did not really care much about God. It was just the practice of religion. I prayed to God mostly at year-end going into the new year. My late husband was similar. When he would take us to church then, he would not enter the church premises, but would stay in the car reading the newspapers. He would then take us back home when the service was over.

It was later when life began to get more complicated that I found the need for God. It wasn't too late, but things would have been far better for me if I had embraced God much earlier. There were certain decisions I would have made differently had God being the guide of my youth.

> I STRONGLY RECOMMEND MAKING GOD THE CENTER OF YOUR LIFE AND YOUR SOURCE FOR ALL YOUR SUPPLIES

I can tell any young person firsthand that waiting till you get into some terrible crisis and misfortune before turning to God is not the wisest thing to do because you would have suffered and may not have enough time to experience the full answer to your prayers for divine intervention. A verse in the Bible rings so clear:

> *Remember now your Creator in the days of your youth, Before the difficult days come, And the years draw near when you say, "I have no pleasure in them".*

Ecclesiastes 12:1

This passage is a wake-up call for anyone in their youth. The "days of your youth" in the passage is both literal and figurative. Figuratively, it is whenever you wake up to the God-need of your life no matter how old you are. There is an African adage that says, *whenever you wake up is your morning* – that is when you will get up to clean up, even if it is 2 o'clock in the afternoon.

So figuratively, the days of your youth represent the season you realize your need for God, waking up to His reality, whether as a young student or an old retiree, or when in crisis or prosperity. God is ready to embrace you at any time and at whatever point because He loves you unconditionally and is patient continually.

Literally however, the passage is talking about remembering God early while you are still physically young. If you want to live long and well and prepare adequately for your latter years, you should start your pursuit of God early. Pushing it forward may become too far or too late - not for Him, but for you to accomplish His plans in your lifetime.

What is this God-factor that makes life more peaceful and prosperous and gives you a head start on your prosperous latter years? Having God gives a reality of security, safety and support. In a world filled with uncertainties, you need an assurance of hope and faith that you can pray to God and He will answer. No matter

> IF YOU WANT TO LIVE LONG AND WELL AND PREPARE ADEQUATELY FOR YOUR LATTER YEARS, YOU SHOULD START YOUR PURSUIT OF GOD EARLY.

how bad things may be, you can turn to God. He will be there. This blessed assurance is worth it all. It may be hard to quantify but having it is the place you want to be as you navigate this life. It gives you courage and strength to forge on.

What I Missed in My Younger Years

As I stated earlier, I was not serious with God when I was younger, but now I have a good and deep relationship with Him. I can tell the difference. Now, prayer is not just asking God to meet my needs. It is communicating with Him. It is a way of expressing our relationship, which gives me further assurance of His support and protection. If I had had such confidence towards God much earlier in life, I would have come through certain things I went through bigger and better. He – God – is a huge factor to how a purposeful and successful life is lived.

Engage the God-Factor Early

O God, You have taught me from my youth; And to this day I declare Your wondrous works. Now also when I am old and gray-headed, O God, do not forsake me, Until I declare Your strength to this generation, Your power to everyone who is to come.

Psalm 71:17-18

It pays to know and serve God. There is a sense of purpose that His knowledge brings. There is a focus that the assurance of His support affords. There is a power that cannot be denied backing His promises. The real and true knowledge of God translates to confidence and courage. Even when things seem to be going bad and awful, the assurance is there that with His grace, things can turn around. In the face of calamity or misfortune, faith in God will keep you going when and where you otherwise would have been stopped. Knowing God and serving Him is a great deal no matter the ups and downs that you may experience in life.

In life, times will arise when you need someone stronger than yourself to carry you. You will need directions when you get to the crossroads that life will most surely present. This is who God is and what He does for those who serve Him.

Seek First the Kingdom

> *Seek first the kingdom of God and His righteousness, and all other things shall be added to you.*

Matthew 6: 33

This passage calls for action. I do not want to force my faith on you if God is not a part of your life, but I am unashamedly a Christian, and if the purpose of this book is to foster a lifestyle that will prevent unwanted outcomes in old age, I cannot exclude God from the equation. He is the major factor.

People often wait for crisis times before calling on God. But this doesn't have to be so. Calling on God early and walking with him can keep you from distress. God is not only a help in crisis, but He is also our shield from crisis.

> IT PAYS TO KNOW AND SERVE GOD. THERE IS A SENSE OF PURPOSE THAT HIS KNOWLEDGE BRINGS. THERE IS A FOCUS THAT THE ASSURANCE OF HIS SUPPORT AFFORDS.

Whether you pray to Him in peace or in crisis, He will answer. Whether you make Him the first option or the last, He will respond to you with compassion. Whether you call on Him early in life or much later, He will walk with you from where you are. When He says you should seek Him early, it is only for your own sake. Know Him and serve Him now.

The quest to advance in life is one that most of us share. We pursue success, accolades, wealth and influence. There is nothing wrong with seeking excellence and being the best we can be in life, but one thing should come first: our pursuit of God. When you make God your first pursuit, all the things that people seek after will be added to you.

To the younger ones, please take this as advice from an elder, speaking from the benefit of hindsight, from personal experiences, and from the Word of God. Please, remember the Lord God in the days of your youth. Never exclude the God-factor. It will make all the difference.

CHAPTER 2

The Work Factor

People who don't use their black hair to work hard will have to work very hard with their grey hair.

- African Adage

I n the last chapter, we discussed the God-factor. It is the central and most important part of your preparation for your golden years. However, it is not the only thing you need to ensure that your preparation is in place. In this chapter, I want to deal with your work.

Not everyone in this world will become a millionaire, but everyone ought to have their basic needs met. It is not God's design for anyone to beg for food or shelter, particularly in old age when physical strength is diminished.

The Inadequacies of Social Safety Nets

It is not a good thing to see older people suffer. That is why the governments of developed countries do their best to take care of their very older citizens through a welfare plan - like social security payments in the United States - in order to ensure that their basic needs are met. I currently work as a caregiver for a 92-year old man who is living on such a plan. However, even social security payments are based on credits you have earned by paying into the system in your working years.

In Africa, we do not have the privilege of such a welfare plan. Back then in Nigeria, I witnessed the sorry state of many pensioners who, after working for 35 years or more, had to be on a long queue to receive their meager monthly checks. I believe things may have changed now with an improved system and electronics bank transfers, but then some would be owed for months by their employers, and with practically nothing to feed and fend for themselves. They had to fall back on family members for succor.

We could blame the government, the system and the employer, but could they have done things differently during those 35 years of active duty to realize a more comfortable life after retirement? I really think so.

> IT IS NOT A GOOD THING TO SEE OLDER PEOPLE SUFFER.

Now, even in America, for many people of retirement age who are still agile, it is still a life of struggle because many of them have to continue doing menial jobs to survive. I know many people in their 70s who still work as much as 7 to 8 hours a day in order to fend for themselves. They are still working so hard because they have bills to pay...

Are You Working Smart for Now and Then?

There are a number of reasons one can point to for this unhealthy state of things, but the one reason this chapter will focus on is that people usually work hard at old age because they did not work smart or hard enough during their younger years.

Don't get me wrong. I do not mean they were not engaged with one work or another in their younger years. Rather, I mean they were not engaged enough for one reason or the other to take care of then and now. The best they did was to live and work for the then present rather than for both the present and future. Whichever way you want to look at it, in my honest opinion, it is a result of laziness – physical or mental.

> THE PRINCIPLE OF WORKING AND COMPENSATION TO TAKE CARE OF NOW AND LATER IS AN IMPORTANT PART OF NATURE AND GOD'S METHODS OF TAKING CARE OF HIS CREATION.

Learn from the Birds and the Ants

There is an adage that says "even though God gives birds their food, He doesn't throw it into their nests."

The principle of working and compensation to take care of now and later is an important part of nature and God's methods of taking care of his creation. Just look at one of the tiniest creatures God created – the ant.

Ants are famous for their diligence in storing food up for the winter time. Solomon advised us to observe and learn from the ants:

Go to the ant, you sluggard!

Consider her ways and be wise,

Which, having no captain,

Overseer or ruler,

Provides her supplies in the summer,

And gathers her food in the harvest.

How long will you [slumber, O sluggard?

When will you rise from your sleep?

A little sleep, a little slumber,

A little folding of the hands to sleep—

So shall your poverty come on you like a prowler,

And your need like an armed man.

Proverbs 6:8-11

Also remember that that next thing God did after placing man in His Garden in Genesis 2 was to inform him of His required responsibilities of work. He gave him an assignment. His work was to take care of the garden. That Garden was provided by God but the man still had to till it and protect it. He had to do some work to get the food that God has provided for him in the garden. Your work is a very important part of living life well and preparing for your future.

No Excuses

Some young people just play away their future. As the popular saying goes, "If you play now, you will pay later." As simple as that sounds, it is a principle that many young people still ignore.

Yes, there are life challenges that make excelling in life an uphill climb, but that is the reason you are endowed with willpower, relationships and the ability to reach out to God for help to find a way to overcome the challenge. When life throws bricks at you, you can either let it destroy you or use the bricks to build a house. Tea does not bring out its flavors until it is put in hot water. No matter how tough and rough your experience is in life, you can overcome the difficulties to realize a great future. No excuses. You can become great in life if you really work hard at it.

I live in America now, and I know there are many black people that have come from abject poverty in Africa who are now doing well in America, even better than many born in America. There are also many children of the poor doing much better than the children of the rich. It is all about determination, vision and hard work.

The Importance of Vision

Many young people today lack vision. I have encountered them both in Africa and America. They just cannot see beyond their noses. They live only for today because their views are clouded by the fads and fashions of the modern day. A young lady of twenty-two years wants to ride an exquisite car or live in the same mansion an accomplished 52-year-old woman is living in? Get to work, my dear young lady! The woman you are trying to copy has had 30 years of hard work behind her, and she has assets she has built up to acquire such a car or property. Work hard when you are young so that you can enjoy the fruits of your hard work later in life.

Vision is very important in life. The vision for financial freedom or to have a great life in the older years should be one the things driving the young, not trying to acquire possessions they cannot afford and assets that will soon become liabilities.

Such a vision of the future makes them do everything possible to achieve their aims or to at least come close to doing so. It will motivate them to burn the proverbial midnight candle, live within their means in order to save for the future, go to school or take professional courses in order to get certified, work longer hours by cutting off the frivolities which many of their contemporaries are caught in. It will motivate them to create multiple sources of income. They will have a source of income and create another stream of income, and create yet another through the passive income they are making.

> NO EXCUSES. YOU CAN BECOME GREAT IN LIFE IF YOU REALLY WORK HARD AT IT.

Many youths today are content with having jobs that are not well-paying. You may start that way but it should not remain that way. If you find yourself in such a situation after working for a while, please wake up to reality! If when you are young, you only have a job that cannot meet your needs, how do you think your needs will be met at old age? What stops you from having another side job or a business apart from your primary job? Who says salaried workers should not do business? Who says business people should not have investment creating passive income? These are some wrong mindsets that keep people from becoming financially buoyant and free.

As a young or middle-aged person, you need to work harder to ensure a plan is in place for your old age so that you will not have to suffer at that time. Put your physical and mental faculties to work now. Find a way to create another stream of income that will improve your living conditions and then afford you a plan for the future.

The reality is that you are responsible for your results and outcomes in life. The government, family and other people can only do a part. It is often said that people that don't use their black hair to work hard will have to work very hard with their grey hair. Don't let that be your story. I think we have enough examples of that around. Please don't add to the numbers. Get on your feet and work hard and smart while you still can. Make hay while the sun   shines!

CHAPTER 3

The Savings Factor

If putting money aside helps in the unexpected, it even helps much more in the expected. Old age is definitely expected, or should be.

\- The Author

There are various statistics on the internet obtained from surveying the saving habits of Americans. One found out that 69% of Americans have less than $1000 in savings. Another reports that half of Americans 55 years or older have nothing saved up for retirement. This explains a lot.

America has statistics but I perceive that this might even be worse for developing nations in Africa that do not do such surveys. It is most likely then a universal fact that in all societies people don't save at all or save enough for their golden years. I want to address this in this chapter.

Cultivating the Habit of Saving

One of the most painful feelings anyone can have is to look back in one's older years and see the many opportunities missed by not setting aside some money from all the incomes received throughout one's younger years. It is often marked by regret at having wasted those opportunities. I want to advise my younger readers to do everything they can to ensure they never get to experience this. No matter how old you are now, it is not too late to start putting something aside.

Saving is a habit that must be cultivated. It is choosing to pay yourself a part of your money which you would naturally pay to others. So, just as you would pay your light bills, rent or mortgage, decide to include yourself and your future as a payee. Your older self will thank your younger self for doing this.

The Benefits of Saving

Saving money is beneficial in many ways. I will share a few of them here:

First, savings allow you to have capital that you can invest or use to start a business. The reason why a lot of people in their prime may not be able to have other streams of income apart from their salaries is because they don't have the culture of savings.

> NO MATTER HOW OLD YOU ARE NOW, IT IS NOT TOO LATE TO START PUTTING SOMETHING ASIDE.

Another benefit of savings is that it helps to curb unnecessary spending. It helps you to live within your means. To save, you would have to watch your expenses. This helps you develop the habit of delaying your desires until the appropriate time. It also ensures that you are keeping your future in mind and prioritizing your expenses to what really matters.

The saving habit also makes you conscious enough to plug the holes that your money needlessly leaks through. Some spending habits are not that important to your survival.

In Nigeria, a country whose economy currently doesn't look so good, with a chunk of the people below the poverty line, you still find people throwing parties to show off, putting themselves into debt they may have to pay through their noses for months and years to come. Some spend more money on a one-day wedding or christening of their baby than they will ever set aside as savings in 35 years of their working life. Sometimes, I wonder if poverty is a state or a mentality. It seems it is more of the latter.

Not saving and living within one's means is the major problem of several people that have to keep working or become excessively dependent on others financially in their old age. Life may not be all rosy, but it offers opportunities to everyone. Saving helps you to cash in on such opportunities.

Saving Vehicles for Retirement

Governments of most countries create avenues for their citizens to save for their retirement. It could be a pension benefit plan, a safety net like Social Security or contributions plans like the IRA or 401(k) in the United States. Such structures make saving and building a reserve much easier - or even compulsory for all whose income comes by an employer's payroll.

SAVING HELPS YOU TO CASH IN ON OPPORTUNITIES.

While it is great to take advantage of this, I also advise that in these times when the economies of many countries in the world are experiencing turmoil, you should also put your destiny in your own hands by setting money aside in your more active years in other forms of savings. Remember your latter years may stretch for several decades so ensure that you calculate what would be enough for you to live comfortably in your less active latter years.

Force Yourself to Save

I know this may be hard to do with all your expenses at the moment, but it is important that you make this happen. Pay yourself first by all means! There may be present worries about what to eat and how to pay bills but you will still have to develop the habit of saving and building a reserve no matter how hard things are. There is no better way to plan for old age from the financial angle than to build a reserve from what one regularly earns long before the retirement age.

Building a reserve is all about saving, and saving is income you did not spend, or deferred consumption that can help you safeguard your future.

Prepare for the "Lean" Years

The Bible gives us an account that illustrates the wisdom of saving. Egypt became the greatest civilization in the ancient world during the time of Joseph. Joseph interpreted Pharaoh's dreams and wisely advised him to save up during seven years of plenty. By the time the seven years of shortage came, the nation had enough to survive on and to excel above other nations that did not plan ahead.

It would be good if you can view your latter years as years of shortage because they will be marked with a fraction of the active earnings you had before, and with less energy and connections to do business. The younger working professional or business person should use the years of plenty while they are still fully working and their income is still tied to their direct in-person work or capabilities to save for the future. A time will come when the capabilities and positions will be greatly reduced or totally lost. Like it happened in Egypt, you need to save for the years of shortage.

Learn Again from The Ant

In the last chapter I made mention of the ant as a hard-worker, but that was not the only thing about the ant that Solomon revealed. He also referred to the fact that the ant lays up food in the summer in preparation for the winter. Summer represents days of activities while winter represents days of reduced activities.

In Chicago, during the summer, the streets are filled with people. Graduations, weddings and other activities are on. Farming activities take place in preparation to be harvested in the fall. The sun shines brightly and the temperature is warm. People go on vacation. There are a lot of activities. But once it is winter, the streets are deserted except for cars. Most things move indoors. Warmth decreases and activities decrease.

This is an illustration of the seasons of our lives. When we are young, it is like summer. Old age is like winter. We must make good use of the summer, in order to be prepared for the winter.

Fruits in Your Latter Years

> *The righteous shall flourish like a palm tree, He shall grow like a cedar in Lebanon. Those who are planted in the house of the Lord Shall flourish in the courts of our God. They shall still bear fruit in old age; They shall be fresh and] flourishing.*

Psalm 92-12-14

Getting old is a reality. It is coming. I am there now, and I can relate with this reality. Thank God for the support of my wonderful children but if you have not prepared during your years of plenty, no matter the support you receive, you may find it difficult to do so much for yourself.

Apart from this, God wants you to be fruitful in old age. He wants you to be able to continue having impact on your family, your church and community. You may be unable to do this if you have not laid aside some resources for those times during your years of plenty.

Present Financial Hardship Makes Savings Even More Important

The challenge for many younger and working individuals is that it doesn't seem to them that they are in their years of plenty, considering their limited incomes and their current expenses. But such a situation only makes savings even more important. Strive to save, even if it is just a little and even when times are tough. Your accumulating amounts will give you a positive feeling of having a capital that can be helpful in changing your financial experiences from scarcity to abundance.

The more you feel you have abundance, the more abundance you attract to yourself. So, saving, even with limited income, will enlarge your ability to save more.

> GOD WANTS YOU TO BE FRUITFUL IN OLD AGE. HE WANTS YOU TO BE ABLE TO CONTINUE HAVING IMPACT ON YOUR FAMILY, YOUR CHURCH AND COMMUNITY.

For whoever has, to him more will be given; but whoever does not have, even what he has will be taken away from him.

Mark 4:25

In conclusion, I want to emphasize that if saving works for the unexpected, it will work even much more for the expected. Old age is expected, or should be. No matter how much you want to wish it away, it will certainly come if your life is preserved. So, prepare for those inevitable years by laying up for them now.

CHAPTER 4

Invest Now for Your Golden Years

If I have one regret in life, it would be that I did not start investing early enough.

- The Author

I wish I had this book in my hands thirty to forty years ago. I would not have passed up many investment opportunities that came along the way. I have always been industrious, from as early as my school days. I was nicknamed "Businesswoman" because I knew how to turn one shilling to two and two shillings to four. I used to loan my dad money to pay my school fees, which he would return later. In my earlier schooling years, I was never sent out of school because of school fees. I was that good with trading.

Ignorance is Costly

But all that didn't eventually count because I really did not know about investing. I used to save but at the end of the year I would break the clay piggy-bank and spend the money on Christmas clothes. I never learned how to invest until much later in life.

> I WISH I HAD THIS BOOK IN MY HANDS THIRTY TO FORTY YEARS AGO. I WOULD NOT HAVE PASSED UP MANY INVESTMENT OPPORTUNITIES THAT CAME ALONG THE WAY.

Several years later, someone asked me if I wanted to buy some shares. I told her I had enough furniture in my house, thinking she was talking about chairs to sit on (Chairs and shares sound almost the same in my native accent).

It shows you how naïve I was back then, and this continued up until middle age. In the same country Nigeria then, a nurse who is a princess - daughter of a renowned king - whom I got to know later, was setting aside Two Hundred Naira every month as savings, which she used largely to buy stocks. Today, the returns on her investment have become so big that she would not need to work again the rest of her life.

To be sincere, this is something I regret. Even if it was just ten percent of that figure a month I had been putting into long-term savings and investments at that time, it would most probably be in the millions now by the worth of that investment. I would have been writing this book as an accomplished investor who has come, seen and conquered in the investment world.

It is not that I am not successful today. I am, but not as much as I want to, and if I could wind time back, read this book and others like it, I would make some better financial decisions. But that is impossible, so I focus on doing this even more aggressively now and encouraging my children, grandchildren and other younger ones.

Again, it is not that I wasn't saving then, but the saving we – the people around me then and I – knew to do was saving for the moment to meet important needs such as paying our yearly rents, fund our children's education and handle other short-term expenses.

As traders, we usually would get ourselves together in a cooperative club or society and make weekly or monthly contributions with every member taking turns to collect the total pooled money monthly. We felt good doing this but we did not know we were only scratching the surface of the benefits of what the savings could do if we had allowed it to grow with interest by investing some of it. We were saving to meet short-term needs alone, and not to secure the long-term.

Time is of Essence

Don't get me wrong. It was good we had savings as an umbrella to shield us from the rain of present bills at that time, but we could have put more efforts into ensuring that we also changed the whole sky over us by creating a bright financial future through investments. How I wish that every worker could come up to the level where they are not just focused on paying bills and meeting needs, but also - and more importantly - securing their old age financially.

This is done by waking up to the practice of investing right early from the moment you begin to earn money. Investments work with compound interest and the maximizing of compound interest requires the factor of time. The longer you practice investing, the more benefits of compounding you will enjoy.

Investing early is also important because investing is not a risk-free venture. There are risks involved, and the longer you have to learn how to navigate the risks in investing - even if it means failing and falling forward on a few occasions - the better. Starting to invest much later in your career or working years (though it is better late than never) is a lot riskier as you may not gain as much as the other guy who started 10 or 20 years before. Also, your aggressiveness in order to make up for lost time can expose you to even more risks.

A late investor is likely to be harder hit if the investment runs into some serious issues. It will be devastating for you to lose a third of the money you saved for retirement a year before retirement. But if you start early and this happens a year or two into your working experience, you still have enough time to bounce back and learn from that misfortune.

(THE LONGER YOU PRACTICE INVESTING, THE MORE BENEFITS OF COMPOUNDING YOU WILL ENJOY.)

Investing Has Perpetual Benefits

Now, this is not to put fear or discouragement in the hearts of those who may be late-starters. I started late myself, and I am getting along pretty well. Now that I know the importance of investment, I would rather invest than not invest because investing not only continues to benefit you for the rest of your life, it can also extend beyond your lifespan to benefit your children and those who come after you. Work may stop but investing continues because it does not necessarily require your physical presence or exertion. You don't need to clock in at 9am and clock out 4pm every working day of the week. It only needs your capital and your brain - or the brain of your broker if you have one.

I began investing with knowledge and focus during the stock market boom in Nigeria between 2005 and 2008 but only got really involved almost at the tail end of the boom, so I couldn't make much profit before the stock market crashed. It however was a real eye-opener for me - that made me to really wonder what I had been doing with my life up until then. More so, the process of investing I was put through by my involvement was enough training to make me look out for more investment opportunities - anywhere and in any form.

When I eventually crossed over to the United States, I was all out looking for one that fits my status and, today, I am finding fulfilment and gain in a savings and investment venture. Better late than never, I repeat. Even in uncertain times, it is better and more important to invest than not to do so. It is one of the surest ways to guard against the financial pressures of the future, particularly after retirement.

Learn from My Story

Do I have any regret in life? It must be the fact that I didn't start investing early in life. I have written this book to tell someone not to make the same mistake. If you are in your 40s or 30s or even 20s, I really envy the fact that you are reading this book at this time. Take it from me, time waits for no one. And with changes and disruptions that may happen across industries, you need to start investing right early to better secure your future and old age.

Retirement, if not planned for, may bring another kind of stress as serious as the stress of work - financial stress. Work may be over after retirement, but living continues, and living requires finances. At a time that you will not have much physical strength to move around, you shouldn't be struggling to fend for yourself. Whether you are in the developed world with social safety nets for its working class or in a developing world that the best out there is a basic pension plan, or you work for a company or have your own business; whether you are a male or a female, you need to take investing so seriously that you start working on it now.

CHAPTER 5

Invest in your Children's Future

The child that you refuse to train because you are building a house will eventually sell for peanuts the house you built.

- African Adage

I remember that as far back as when I was a teenager, I made a solemn decision that I would do everything within my powers to ensure that my children would be educated up to the university level. I did not have that privilege myself of going to college because my own parents were formally uneducated.

Invest in Your Children's Education

My father was a farmer, and in those days, children were expected to help their parents on the farm, and by my father's reasoning, there was no point in putting in all the efforts in sending me to school beyond the basic education levels.

I really desired to go further in my formal education but had to yield to my father's wishes. I saw some of his friends sending their own children to grammar school, and I remembered how I vowed then that I would send my own children to school to the highest levels possible even if I had to sell all my possessions to get it done. Looking back now, I am glad I was able to accomplish this without having to sell all my properties. I delivered well on that goal. I encourage all parents to strive to deliver on this as well.

Don't Make Your Children Your Financial Security Plan for Old Age

I would however like to sound this note of warning to those just raising their own children: Getting your children educated as an investment for old age may be a premise that may not work so much again. Many parents of my generation back then in Nigeria saw sending their children to school as a way of securing their latter years. Well, it is not a bad plan, because the children you really cared for when they were young - who know your sweat was part of what brought them to a life of success - will want to do everything to return that care in your old age. But don't bank on this because life has changed. That template is being eroded by the realities of today's world. Many children who would love to support their parents substantially are unable to do so because of their own personal and family needs. The realities of life these days may be so demanding on their finances that even though they care, they may only be able to support to an extent that does not fully meet all your needs.

In my own parenting days back then in Nigeria, once your child graduates from school, a plum job would be waiting for him. Today, a graduate in Nigeria may still be on the streets five years after graduation desperately seeking employment. How would someone without a job or income come to the rescue of his parents? How easy is it for someone whose business just got hit by a crisis to meet all the needs of his parents?

Today's parents who are still seeing their children through school must wise up and make the necessary mind-shift so they will not be disappointed in their old age.

Education is An Investment in Your Children, Not Yourself

Is education – sending your children to school – not an investment? Yes, it is, but it is an investment for the children, not necessarily the parents. I understand how much it could cost a parent to educate a child all the way through college, but the main reward should be the sheer joy and fulfilment that you have provided the child a great pedestal to build a successful life on. This endeavor will even be much easier if you have a plan of financial investment right from the birth of the child – or even before.

> TODAY'S PARENTS WHO ARE STILL SEEING THEIR CHILDREN THROUGH SCHOOL MUST WISE UP AND MAKE THE NECESSARY MIND-SHIFT SO THEY WILL NOT BE DISAPPOINTED IN THEIR OLD AGE.

A couple I knew back in Nigeria wanted to have a party for their one-year old baby. When the wife gave the husband the budget for the party, the husband insisted that he preferred investing that money to buy shares in the child's name rather than wasting it on a lavish birthday party. He told his wife to go ahead and spend the money she had for the birthday and to remember to take pictures of the event. He informed her that it would be great to see which of the two the child will be more grateful for in 20 years – the birthday pictures or the appreciated investment.

The wife may not have been happy with her husband's decision but I am sure she will be happy years down the line that her husband made such a wise decision on behalf of their child.

In Nigeria, it is a custom that parents have christening ceremonies for their children. People who attend then give cash gifts to the child being christened. If those gifts are invested right away, by the time the child turns eighteen, the investment may have grown enough to meet a level of the child's college expenses. It means that with some good planning, funding the education of children does not have to be a backbreaking financial experience for parents.

Be Hands-On in Your Children's Education

Apart from funding their education, parents should also be personally involved as much as they can in their children's education. Guiding a child according to their bend is so necessary these days in order to provide them a greater chance for success.

Guide them Along Their Bends

WITH SOME GOOD PLANNING, FUNDING THE EDUCATION OF CHILDREN DOES NOT HAVE TO BE A BACKBREAKING FINANCIAL EXPERIENCE FOR PARENTS.

In the tough terrain this world has become, it is important for each person to tap into their unique abilities and strengths in order to succeed. Every child has some unique combinations of strength or learning bend that is natural to them. Some children are academically inclined; others are technically inclined, while some others are artistically inclined, and so on.

Parents must observe the children to know the path each child tends towards and provide support and direction along that path. And when it gets to the point of choosing a career, a career counselor could help the child in choosing the right discipline to major in according to that bend. The area of learning bend is where the child's energy and passion will be expressed the most.

Nurture Their Intelligence

There is also the aspect of helping to nurture the intelligence of your children. Two areas come to mind so strongly regarding this - finances and relationships. Financial intelligence is so essential for a growing child at this time so they can know the value of money and other assets and can begin the process of wealth creation.

So, the parents don't only save and invest themselves, but they also teach their children right early how to do the same. My 14-year-old grandson, Joshua, is already into shares and stocks. His dad taught him. He also sells snacks on Sundays (I am his supplier) making little profit on top, which he can save and invest over time. He also rents shoes to his mates at school.

The development of people skills is also crucial to the child's success in life. The ability to open up discussions, to negotiate, and generally relate with people in meaningful friendships and teamwork is essential.

In addition, children should be encouraged to develop interest in technology. How else will they survive in a tech-ruled world? The reality is that the younger ones already have keen interest in technology because that is all they have come to know. Millennials are unfamiliar with the gramophone or typewriter or even land-based telephones. They only know smartphones, laptops, apps and video games.

Parents and grandparents must be careful not to discourage their children's use of technology because they are not familiar with it. Technology is the future. Even if you have to be a farmer now, you must be a high-tech farmer to fully maximize the potential of your venture.

Discipline Your Children

One last thing I would like to discuss about investing in your children is discipline. This is also so vital because the world will continue to battle with indiscipline and crime. There is an old adage of my native tribe that the child you refuse to train or discipline will sell the house you built for peanuts.

Make the world's problem one less by ensuring your children are well brought up. People often debate about what mode of discipline is best for today's children. But there ought to be little or no argument about it when you consider the goal behind discipline, which is correction. That goal separates discipline from abuse or physical assault. Different societies have differing disciplinary measures they permit. Find ways and measures to correct your children within the confines of the law of the country you live in. Remember to always discipline for correction and not punishment.

CHAPTER 6

Invest in People

"Lonely is one."

- Masai Proverb

As I stated earlier, I work as a caregiver for a nonagenarian, and I can tell it tends to get lonelier and lonelier as one gets older. Not having people to relate with is one issue, but being abandoned or not accepted by the younger generation can be debilitating. Loneliness can lead to worse things like depression, and depression is a killer. It kills before it actually kills. If not dealt with, it kills slowly but steadily.

Depressive symptoms such as withdrawal, anxiety, lack of motivation and sadness may be too much for an older person to bear, and with nobody or nothing to turn to, they may turn to alcohol or cigarettes. Then the door may be opened to a silent death through stroke or heart disease. Or the individual may become a waiting victim for a deadly infection that breaks out. No wonder the people mostly affected when there is an epidemic are older people.

Dealing with Loneliness in Old Age

Part of the cure for loneliness is wholesome fellowship with people, so the way you can prepare against loneliness in your latter years is to build good relationships.

> DEPRESSIVE SYMPTOMS SUCH AS WITHDRAWAL, ANXIETY, LACK OF MOTIVATION AND SADNESS MAY BE TOO MUCH FOR AN OLDER PERSON TO BEAR

In countries like America where citizens can be very individualistic, people often keep to themselves. Neighbors may not speak to one another for months. However, if you want to live and prepare well for your latter years, you should make it a practice to build relationships. You must be strategic about building good and lasting relationships with several people, bearing in mind that you may lose some of those people to death along the way as you grow older.

Build Relationships with Those Younger Than You

It also means you must build relationships with younger ones. This requires an important skill - the ability to find common ground. You will not be able to build relationships with many young people if you cannot come down to their level.

I am often called the mother of nations by those who know me very well because I deliberately make it a consistent practice to relate with people particularly those younger than me. I have many children both in Africa and America that I did not give birth to because I am involved in many lives. They have come to love and respect me for this. They are also committed to me as much as I am committed to them.

Build Relationships to Impact Lives

The purpose of building such relationships is to impact lives. And that is what I have done and still continue to do. There are so many individuals that can trace good decisions they made and the action they took due to my input one way or the other. Just in the place I currently live in, I have gained so many "children" this way. I use my smiles, cheers, words of encouragement or prayer to serve people.

> I DELIBERATELY MAKE IT A CONSISTENT PRACTICE TO RELATE WITH PEOPLE PARTICULARLY THOSE YOUNGER THAN ME.

The primary benefit of my gesture for me is not material but deeper than that. It is a sense of fulfillment that comes from doing good to others. The feeling may be hard to explain, but when you are blessing others, there is a way you feel good about yourself that you don't get bogged down with your own problems. That sense of fulfillment - coupled with the faith that whatever I make happen for others God will make happen for me – keeps me going always and keeps away worry and anxiety about life's concerns.

The Reciprocity of Investing in People

Also, touching others keeps good and trusted people around me. This helps keep loneliness away. As I get older, I continue to add more people into my circle to talk and relate with.

One day, a daughter of mine whom I have won over through my loving care, visited the 92-year old man I worked for. The old man was amazed because she thought she was my real daughter. He asked me how I was able to keep the relationship going between her and myself because the more common thing in America is that people that old would have been neglected by the younger ones.

The Keys to Imparting Lives

Well, there is no special secret there other than this: If you want to have friends, you must show yourself friendly. Whoever cares enough to be a friend, sister, brother, mother, father to others will have friends, sisters, brothers, mothers and fathers that are not related to them by blood. It is the law of cause and effects!

How do you start the journey of imparting lives? Get interested in what interest others. You can also build more relationships by becoming an active member of a community or religious group. I am a widow. Apart from the very good relationship I have with my children that is as strong as ever, I have been in the last three decades an active member in my church both back in Nigeria and now in the United States. That is where I have been able to draw many friends - older, younger and also agemates. I belong to a department in church and members work together and look out for one another. I do catering, and many of my customers and referrals are from my relationships in church. Guess where I launched this book and who were the first buyers and readers? Members of my church! What a blessing to be part of a functional group where members are loving, forgiving, dutiful and forging ahead together!

I can categorically state that I will always have good and loving people around me till my very old age and until I breathe my last. Why?

Because I have impacted many lives already and have built many great relationships as a result. The simple rule here is to keep your old relationships as much as you can and to keep making new ones. Keep adding to your company of friends. Don't keep to yourself in the name of minding your own business. If someone tells you to mind your business, meaning you should not talk or relate with people, tell them you are doing just that (minding your business). Your business actually is to build relationships and touch lives.

> KEEP YOUR OLD RELATIONSHIPS AS MUCH AS YOU CAN AND TO KEEP MAKING NEW ONES.

Are you in your 30s and 40s now – or even your 20s or 50s? How well have you done in building relationships? How many lives have you impacted? You may need to really think about this now. How well is the giving and receiving going on between you and the people close to you? If it is not strong enough, you may have to give more so that people around you can begin to feel that you are an indispensable part of their lives. Just make sure your relationships are built on mutual values. Join a group with similar values as yours and make other families a part of your own family – of course, do not neglect your biological children, siblings and their family as well.

Family is a blessing – whether biological or social! Family exists so that members can be there for one another. There may be some hurts or betrayals along the way, but that is not enough reason to stop relating with people because the gains far outweigh the pains. Part of the gain is that you will not be lonely in your old age – if you have built your relationships so well and have created families for yourself in addition to your biological family.

When you are older, you are more vulnerable to various ailments including loneliness. Many suicide cases are as a result of depression caused by loneliness. When there is no one to talk to, loneliness can happen. That is why you should ensure that you build a big family of trusted people and well-wishers. The rude reality is if you become so lonely – now or later in life – we need to ask you, "Where is your family?" So, don't wait till you are old before you realize you never built relationships that will serve you as a senior. Get to work now and build your own village

through building relationships and imparting
others.

CHAPTER 7

Practice a Healthy Lifestyle

A man too busy to take care of his health is like a mechanic too busy to take care of his tools.

- Unknown

I have observed how people who were strong when they retired suddenly grew so old, and died soon a few years after retiring. My late husband experienced this. In his younger years, he was one of the strongest people I knew. His only ailments were a couple of headaches. He was a very active man. But shortly after his retirement, he became less active, and soon started experiencing certain illnesses. He passed away at 76 from complications of one of these illnesses. May God rest his soul.

It is important that we remain active. Retirement for me does not mean tired, but taking things rather more slowly so I don't overexert myself physically. Work does not have to stop after retirement. Though I am over 70 years, I still work both in my church and as a caregiver and caterer. This is not necessarily for my financial upkeep but more for my physical and mental wellbeing. Apart from the fact that my catering enterprise (catering is a lifetime hobby of mine) has extended into retirement, I also work a few hours three days a week as a caregiver. This helps me to be regularly engaged mentally and physically, and I use it as a means of exercise as well.

> RETIREMENT FOR ME DOES NOT MEAN TIRED, BUT TAKING THINGS RATHER MORE SLOWLY SO I DON'T OVEREXERT MYSELF PHYSICALLY.

My caregiver duty allows me to go out regularly, walking a part of the journey to and fro. The limited working hours allow me to still have time for my catering engagements when I have some supplies to make. And there is still time to rest. I can say that, for my age, I try to have a good balance of resting and exercising – as well as eating.

Eat Healthy

There is an adage in my native language that says, 'Food is the friend of the skin and of facial beauty.' This means if you eat well, it should show in your physical looks. Good nutrients are very important to the body. It is even more critical as you grow older. From age 30, you must mind what, when and how you eat. A balanced meal will not only have starch and protein, but also fruits and vegetables. Fruits and vegetables give us vitamins, and it is vitamins that help boost the immune system of the body against infectious diseases. You should therefore realize that you can actually eat your way into fair health in old age by eating a diet high in fruits and vegetables. You won't have to grow old to become a health liability to your family or the state.

Drink Water

Part of the requirements for a healthy life is water. There are a thousand and one drinks available out there to get you refreshed, but none will do your body as much good as water. Watch out for sugary drinks. Sugar should be reduced to the minimum so as not complicate your health. Rather, drink water regularly enough to make your urine to be pale yellow and not brown.

As you grow older, you may begin to lose the urge to drink as your body may not signal thirst well enough, so, you need to develop a water-drinking routine or schedule right from middle age to keep you taking water even if you don't feel thirsty.

Avoid Taking Toxic Substances

Besides sugar, keep away from alcohol and tobacco because they have so many negative effects on your body. Smoking tobacco cigarettes comes with a strong warning even from the government. The warnings that "tobacco smoking is dangerous to health" and "smokers are liable to die young" should not be taken lightly. Another adage from my native African tribe says indulgence kills more surely than poverty. Don't kill yourself before your time.

The unfortunate thing about indulging in tobacco and alcohol is that one could easily get addicted to them, resulting in silly habits and an unhealthy lifestyle difficult to overcome even when you know they are dangerous. You know you are slowly killing yourself, but you still cannot find the strength to stop the habits. That is how bad addiction to alcohol and tobacco can be.

> INDULGENCE KILLS MORE SURELY THAN POVERTY. DON'T KILL YOURSELF BEFORE YOUR TIME.

However, with a fresh vision to live well and to prepare well for your latter years, you may seek necessary external help to break the hold if you are already addicted. The best thing is not to be in such a situation at all, so if you are not yet addicted, keep away from alcohol and tobacco for your own sake.

Practice Moderation

Health, they say, is wealth, and having a healthy lifestyle is important if you want to live long and well. Moderation must therefore be your watchword. You cannot afford to eat at the same rate as a 25-year-old if you are nearing 50 or 60. It is not only what you eat but how and when you eat it. You cannot afford to eat heavily at odd hours no matter how balanced the meal. The kind of exercise you also do must be age-appropriate. As you grow older, you will need to do more aerobic exercises than anaerobic ones, and may need to cut your exercise down to brisk-walking or strolling.

Get in the Habit of Exercising

Exercise helps to keep the body - particularly the heart and lung - healthy. The average human being can have a healthier body by keeping the organs, tissues and bones engaged through exercise without putting undue stress on these body parts. For the young and old, walking is a beneficial exercise for keeping the body in shape.

Practice Resting

Lastly, you need to rest more as you grow much older. Naturally, your body needs a lot of it. Sleep is good. It helps you to deal with stress, keep a healthy weight, lower your risks for serious health problems and make you think more clearly.

So, as you grow older, sleep and rest come in handy. Just don't make it about sleep alone, so you will not age unnecessarily. As you grow older, have the right balance of sleep, exercise and diet. All things being equal, you will keep a healthy body system and shape that way, even at old age.

Lack of exercise kills. Bad eating habits kill. Stress kills. These may not kill as fast as a deadly virus, but they sure are slow and steady killers.

My advice to anyone, even those young enough to be my children, is to start working towards having a healthy body in old age by having a healthy lifestyle from now as described in this chapter. Develop these habits while you are young and keep growing in them.

CHAPTER 8

Trust in God

Never be afraid to trust an unknown future to a known God.

- Corrie Ten Boom

I contemplate life as I write this final chapter. Strong feelings well up within me as I think of the grace of God. Everyone my age can identify with the fact that many that they started life with have already passed on. I can testify to that. Some of these people were more educated, wealthier, younger, fitter or more renowned than I am. Some were people you would say deserve to eat the fruits of their labors in their old age but who by a stroke of misfortune left this world prematurely.

If I am still alive and well and have the ability to write such a book as this to prepare the coming generation for their older years, I reckon that it is only by the grace of God and I give Him all the glory for it.

The point I am making as I wrap up this book is that life comes with its challenges. It is full of crisis and misfortunes. There are some misfortunes that could be avoided, but some are purely accidental. You may not be able to plan against the occurrence of certain things as we live in a fallen world. The only place of succor is to trust in the grace of God and his divine protection and intervention.

Most of the previous chapters of this book dealt with the natural ways of preparing well for your golden years and steps to prevent unwanted outcomes. The practices advised are good and necessary. This is why they make the bigger portion of this book. However, as I stated in the first chapter, the God-factor is the most critical because we are to live under his grace.

Can God keep you from certain accidents or misfortunes? Well, He won't be God if He cannot. Even many who deny the existence of God call upon Him for help when they are in deep trouble. Can God enable a long and well-lived life with all the provisions necessary in old age? I say He can, based on His numerous promises in the Bible. The Bible has several passages that God promised to protect, preserve and provide for you. Enjoying these were always tied to faith and trust in Him.

> IF I AM STILL ALIVE AND WELL, I RECKON THAT IT IS ONLY BY THE GRACE OF GOD AND I GIVE HIM ALL THE GLORY FOR IT.

Again, it may be difficult for you to trust and believe in God if the picture you have of Him is not so clear. But could this be because we have not been able to embrace the truths about Him?

We are the ones in need of divine support and intervention. We are the ones at His mercy, yet He waits patiently on us to come to a level of faith so that He can do for us what His promises have already declared. His promises are good enough because He is not a man that lies.

God's promises should serve as an anchor for you as you journey through life. He won't be God if He can't make a promise and fulfil it. When you trust God and believe in His promises about long life and prosperity, you put yourself in a position to ensure His grace works on your behalf.

Accidents and misfortunes that could terminate your life or break your back financially will be kept away from you. Why? God will not allow you to be tempted above what you can bear. That is a promise of scripture.

Sounds unreal? That is the way spiritual things sound. They sound untrue, as if someone is making them up. Yes, there are natural principles and laws regarding anything in life including living long and ending well, but there are also spiritual laws and principles.

These two sets of laws complement one another, working hand in hand. Your belief in God should not stop you from doing the natural things it takes to prepare well for your old age. Conversely, your practice of the natural principles should not make you lose trust in God. Only God can keep you from misfortunes that your planning couldn't cover.

Draw near to God. He is your ultimate security in life. Make your plans for life and old age without neglecting His grace. Don't wait until things have almost gone out of hand before seeking Him. He would still answer you, but you may have suffered needlessly. As I stated in the first chapter, now is the time to remember the Lord your God. This is the best time to start seeking Him and developing your relationship with Him, not tomorrow.

> ONLY GOD CAN KEEP YOU FROM MISFORTUNES THAT YOUR PLANNING COULDN'T COVER.

Get grounded in God. Become more aware of His promises. Get established in the truth that He wants you to live a prosperous and fulfilled life from beginning to end. Trust that His grace covers your entire lifespan. Keep yourself reminded of these promises:

> *With long life will I satisfy him, and show him My salvation.*
> **Psalm 91:16**

Beloved, I pray that you may prosper in all things and be in health, just as your soul prospers.
3 John 2

Do all you can in the natural then rest on the promises of God. He will not fail you – because He always keeps His word. Go forth and lead a life of greatness from your youth and through your golden years. I love you.

ABOUT THE BOOK

The old often look back and wonder how their youthful days went by so quickly, and many regret the missed opportunities of their prime years. The younger ones often live largely oblivious of the rapid approach of their latter years, neglecting to plan adequately for them.

In *Caution! Old Age Ahead,* Septuagenarian Beatrice Ijiwola shares passionately and transparently with the young from her own life experiences and from insights gained through extensive interactions with fellow seniors in the two continents she has lived - Africa and North America.

She passes on practical wisdom on how the younger ones, with more years ahead of them than they have lived, can adequately prepare now to secure a comfortable life without lack or regrets in old age. She also shares how her contemporaries - grandparents, retirees and other seniors - who may feel they hit their latter years without adequate preparations - can regain a measure of fulfillment. Readers, young and old, who heed the practical advice in this book will learn how to make what usually is the loneliest, weakest and least independent season of life into one of great productivity, fulfilment and joy.

ABOUT THE AUTHOR

Beatrice Ijiwola has had some unchanging passions throughout her life: entrepreneurship, business, creatively combining recipes to make food, and solving problems by lending listening ears and sharing godly wisdom and resources with those around her.

A natural leader and entrepreneur, after being successful for three decades at running her own restaurant, her quest for another of her passion – empowering people with transformative truth – led her to attend the Word of Faith Bible Institute in Lagos, Nigeria, after which she started using her gift of service in the ministry of her then church, Winners Chapel.

She has since moved to Chicago where she currently resides and serves as a minister at The CityLight Church, founded by one of her sons.

While continuing to run her food catering business and also serving as a care-giver to older citizens, she ministers within and beyond the church walls through her intercessory ministry, hospitality and godly guidance to the younger generation.

Beatrice, a septuagenarian, highly beloved by many, is fondly called "mother of nations" or simply "grandma' by her biological children and grandchildren and numerous adopted children and godchildren spanning the continents of the world.

Made in the USA
Middletown, DE
13 September 2022

73123420R00056